Ugly Time

Sarah Galvin

UGLY

Sarah

TIME

Galvin

GRAMMA
POETRY

UGLY
TIME

Sarah Galvin

Ugly Time

by Sarah Galvin

Printed and bound in USA

Published by Gramma Poetry

www.gramma.press

ISBN 978-1-5323-2705-6

First printing

Distributed by Small Press Distribution

www.spdbooks.org

Cover Image :

Skyspace Bouncehouse © 2007 Mungo Thomson

Acknowledgments

The Author

for Mary Anne

ON DESIGN

It's an ugly time to be alive.
All day, two enormously fat guys
stand on the corner outside my apartment, smoking,

but I'm so distracted by the hideous condo that has just gone up next door
I can't watch them
while I masturbate.

THE SONG ABOUT BEING A PERSON

A doctor instructed me to do a stretch that involves flattening a line of ants with my ass. She was very specific—"Not spiders or beetles," she insisted. She almost certainly prescribed the stretch because she is sexually excited by ants. Under her white coat she was probably covered in them. I don't think less of her as a doctor because of this, I relate to her more as a person. In fact it reminds me of the chorus from that Bob Dylan song about being a person, that goes, "It would bring me to orgasm if my cock were covered in ants."

IRELAND

I want to go to Ireland, but only the Ireland
as represented by this six pack of Irish ale—
rectangles of green obstructed
only by images of wheat
and Celtic knots 10.5 centimeters in diameter.

I'd like to be mentally ill,
but only as it's shown in that movie scene
of the artist's apartment
covered in unfinished paintings
that all look promising—

the only stuff broken in the room
is a shapeless lamp
and a machine that might
be a projector but is probably
an obsolete rice cooker.

I want to go to a country
divided into six neat compartments
each designed to fit
a good thing perfectly.

THE GHOST OF CHRISTMAS PRESENT

I sweated and shook from opium withdrawals
while children frolicked around me
trying to spell the word "boner" with sparklers.

The withdrawals were awful.
It was awful that it was Christmas,
but the sparklers took it to another level

of awful, called "beauty."

Like you step in human shit
while filming porn
and notice the cherry petals
floating like sparks around you.

I knew a boy who intentionally scarred his face
because it was too pretty. I thought he was stupid,
but I understand what he was going for.

THERE'S AN EROTIC NOVEL ABOUT THE TALKING PAPERCLIP FROM WINDOWS 95

I pick the scabs on my neck when I feel anxiety, unless I'm anxious about the scabs, in which case I go down on Hillary Clinton. She is more phobic of scabs than any media entity, except possibly for Mrs. Butterworth, whose lower body is unfortunately made entirely of syrup. When my neck is between Hillary's thighs, she can't see the scabs. I was still surprised this fact enticed her to my 100-square-foot apartment, especially since "Your thighs will obscure my neck wounds" remains the only thing I've said to her. Sometimes when she finishes, all my scabs are gone. Media entities are just regular people in the sense that there's no evidence they're not imaginary. For instance, there's an entire erotic novel about Clippy, the talking paperclip mascot from Windows 95. When you find the erogenous parts of a corporate logo, all of your scabs disappear, and also all of your blood.

WHY "LEXICON DEVIL" BY THE GERMS IS BETTER THAN THE ENTIRE INDIE GENRE

From building a garage-sized house wallpapered with gay porn I learned I can do anything. This may be why I tried to kill Donald Trump with my house keys, a self-defense technique I learned from Oprah. I was frustrated to discover they would barely break the skin, though everyone at the bus stop chanted "STAB HARDER! STAB HARDER!" Oprah said "No, do it like this," and we both stabbed and stabbed. From the window of a café, my most depressed ex's most depressing music came on at an excessively high volume. The tone could not have been less appropriate— we felt like we were in an indie movie about estranged family members reconnecting. To finish him off, we had to hold hands with children dressed in 1980's tennis tracksuits. "Doing anything" has a wider range of meanings than Muppets would have you believe.

A NONZERO NUMBER

How many people have fallen out the window of my apartment? It's an old room with a big window, so probably at least a prosthetic leg? I'm exhausted by buildings so new it seems impossible, with one body, to have enough sex or produce enough corpses to even prove they exist. To stand in such a place feels like floating in an invisible bathtub. I like to live places people have left in every possible trajectory.

I HEARD SHE WAS FIRED
FROM CATHOLIC ARBY'S

But I looked all over that place and couldn't find Arby anywhere.
Maybe this is why I feel what I've heard is called "malaise."

I climbed every historic building in town
and nothing was on top of them.
Now most of them have been demolished
to make way for buildings that lack
even the possibility of something on top of them.

That lack is worse than disappointment.
It's depleting my vitamin D.

To someone with a vitamin deficiency,
human genitalia is invisible.
Nothing is more erotic
than confirming by touch the existence
of something you can't see
except when it's just what you expect.

THE GUTTER ON THE
HOUSE OF MY LIFE

Time is the gutter on the house of my life,
draining away all my non-sexy memories.
I thought I had one non-sexy memory,
of riding a speedboat between two yachts
that were so close together they ripped the hull off the speedboat,

but someone told me recently this actually happened
to Indiana Jones. I was disappointed until I realized that if
I generate enough sexy memories to clog the gutter,
I may become immortal.

POLITICIANS

I told them not to use
the drinking fountain
in the corner,

because when I was in the corner,
the only liquid I could produce
was gasoline.

LIKE THESE THINGS

I told the Like the volume of black still framed by the disintegrating windows of a power plant unused for decades, like the map of Africa in the spreading water stain on the ceiling of the movie theater in by the house I grew up in, like the guy in a Looney Tunes T shirt sprawled in the doorway of a convenient store as if he's been dropped out a second story window, the vivid color of his face and arms, his pink cheek flattened against the sidewalk. I am just like these things lying in bed with you again while you sleep. I'm exactly like these things but stupider, like if they were incorporated in an energy drink commercial.

LIABILITY RUBBER

On a sherbet-colored fall day in Pratt Park
kids climb the jungle gym like the ants
that colonized Jasmine's bra
when she poured candy corn
down her dress at a party.

I heard a story on NPR about a guy who could
orgasm from peeing in the sink.
This plastic jungle gym is composed entirely
of safety features.
Its springy rubber substrate won't prepare
children to fall on an adult sidewalk.

We discourage kids
from participating in reality—
dad banged on the door
as his son came in the sink
to pull him away from the freeway
that's the closest thing
to a jungle gym in this town.

THE MOUNTAIN OF
PILLOWS AND OPTIMISM

What am I, Santa Claus?
Some insist I can't be, because
my penis is made of plastic.
Some say it's possible because I'm white.

When I interviewed for the Santa position,
I laughed at my detractors because
I was the only one present
whose cock wasn't edible.

Laughing at cannibalism
certainly places me within
the Christian mythological tradition.
Fifty years ago, it was legal
for Santa to come down your
chimney any night and eat
your entire family.

I hope my aversion to familial murder
is the reason I didn't get the job.

There's a photo of my grandpa
holding hands with Martin Luther King Jr.,
the same grandpa who told his son
that his earring marked him
as a faggot in every port.

I dreamed I sat with my grandpa
and everyone else in the world
on a mountain of pillows.
No one gave presents
or wanted them.
It was the only place I've ever felt
comfortable with silence.

THERE'S WALDO

Tonight the ghosts that haunt
my apartment materialized.

A severed head lay in my bed,
and all the flying shadows became opaque.

A figure appeared in the doorway—
red-and-white striped shirt, knit cap with a pompom—.

It was Waldo, from Where's Waldo.

I yelled, "There's Waldo! I found him!"
He smiled and waved.

Here, of all places, when I expected to be
accosted by the restless dead—.

I was so happy that insanity manifests itself
this way in my life, and not as racism.

GARFIELD AND FRIENDS, A COMIC BY JIM DAVIS

"It's Monday and you can either make love or die at the hands of the Cobra Commander," is what I would say if I were Garfield. The statement "I hate Mondays," neither proposes an alternative to Mondays or a means of dealing with them. I want at least to give people options, even if the best option involves a human-sized cat box.

THERE IS A WOMAN
WITH A SPECIAL TALENT

She can always tell when someone is screaming. It doesn't
matter who it is, or where they are, or what language they
speak. She can tell by the volume of their voice. I read about
her in the newspaper. All I can think about is her body, but
it's not my fault—the photo of her in the newspaper was only
of her cunt. They did the same thing for that story about the
earthquake.

I ROLL AROUND WEARING ONLY A POWDERED WIG UNTIL ALL OF THE WOUNDS ARE DRY

I turned the daily practice of pulling old pieces of metal out of my skin in the shower into popular dance called the Macarena. I adapted the hard wince and ensuing shudders into a twist followed by a dip. Deeming the rest of the dance's inspiration not fun enough to be a dance, the rest is mostly hand-claps and ass maneuvers. The dance swept the nation, though apparently there was already a dance called the Macarena. Now after recycling the bits of metal each morning I roll around the floor of my apartment wearing only a powdered wig, yelling "I'm George fucking Washington" until I don't care there was already one of those, too.

THE CIVIL WAR

When I can't do something
like remember a sequence of numbers,
or pay attention to board games,
or have a car,
it's because I'm reliving
childhood trauma.
It's like a civil war re-enactment,
my obsessive recollection of how each person fell,
the morphine, the bayonets—
but when you see the hats
you'll totally understand why the whole thing started.

NEIGHBORHOOD VERSUS CONTAINER

She says Greenwood is full of pedophiles and child molesters, I say it's full of motels and restaurants. The argument went on for days. Finally, we put everything in Greenwood into sterile bags, and sent the bags to the University for study. The letter we received a month later stated that because Greenwood is a "neighborhood" and not a "container," it is impossible for it to be "full" of anything, but they thanked us for all the bags that had sex workers in them. Some call sex workers the gasoline that powers research.

MY TWO-DIMENSIONAL FRIEND

Inconveniently the hotel room looks out on another hotel that has come to symbolize despair, but it's comforting knowing someone is having a good time in the room where I stayed, and also to pretend Fidel Castro was a good friend of mine, and that I'm upset he's dead, and continue to add details until it's clear I'm referring to a different celebrity, most often a cartoon. I began doing this years before he died—a lot of things symbolize despair to me.

MID-DAY COWBOY

When I discovered the ever-anticipated kegger with fireworks was a birthday party for the only person who has ever betrayed me, I thought, "If I were a cowboy, I'd just shoot him." I wished and wished I was a cowboy. But then, I noticed someone across the street had put a sign in the window of their apartment that said "life is good," so I went to QFC, and had them make me a cake that said "Happy Birthday Sarah Galvin," and I took all my clothes off and lay on top of it, yelling "Yee haw!" until I was arrested.

WHAT I REMEMBER
ABOUT BEING ARRESTED

Most of my dangerous and irrational behavior has been motivated by asses, yet on the only occasion when I was arrested, the involvement of asses was minimal. The police officer who handcuffed me probably had an ass, but I barely remember. This may have been the worst thing about getting arrested.

"THE STREET LIGHT TODAY IS AN ANGEL OF THE LORD"

—RICHARD KENNEY

Because you had never seen a seagull,
your description of the one
that flew into the store where you work
inspired the manager to call the police.

I want everything to be like that bird,
so overwhelmingly itself
that it is its own spotlight,

but 90% of things are the guy sitting next to me
who punctuates statements like
"I'll put together some numbers for you,"
by pounding the table so hard my coffee bounces.

His animation lacks
the meaning or emotion it references,
like an elaborate set with no play.

There are so many sets.
The absence of a play seems like an emergency,
considering the amount of wasted resources,

but there's not really anyone to call
about this kind of emergency,
which perhaps is why people pray.

EVERYTHING IS COMPOSED EITHER OF MATTER OR LURID SECRETS

One morning, it happened—
I was the millions of Americans who fall
victim to identity theft.
My limbs were a blur
and my social security number
was a long black rectangle.

I had a foot fetish, but
being millions of people,
there was no foot big enough to satisfy me.
The most pornographic things were huge
spaces, because I could imagine feet
that filled their dimensions.

When I looked at the sky,
I was exquisitely still,
overflowing with blankness.

GOLF COURSE

Vibrations are infinite, so every time you slap an ass, your appreciation of that ass is etched into the universe forever. This intersection of sex and math is where I'd expect to find the erogenous parts of concepts, but somehow they are nowhere to be seen. Every object designed by a human is in some way a device for intimacy with the abstract. The longer I live, the more convinced I am that every object is invisibly but outrageously effective, except for manicured lawns. Every time you obsessively mow your lawn, the realm of the abstract is waiting for you to fall asleep so it can masturbate.

GAME SHOW

On a Japanese game show, I made everyone come—the host, the audience, the other contestants, myself—because I was in love. By the time I had finished, I was nearly dead. It was no longer either a game or a show, so no one knew when to stop filming.

SOUND HOLE

I have trouble connecting with people because while I look human, I have the perspective and emotions of a rubber band ukulele. Someone says, "I feel devastated," and I reply, "I emit amusing twanging sounds when the rubber bands stretched across my paper aperture vibrate." I could lie to help people relate, but the defining characteristic of rubber band ukuleles is honesty.

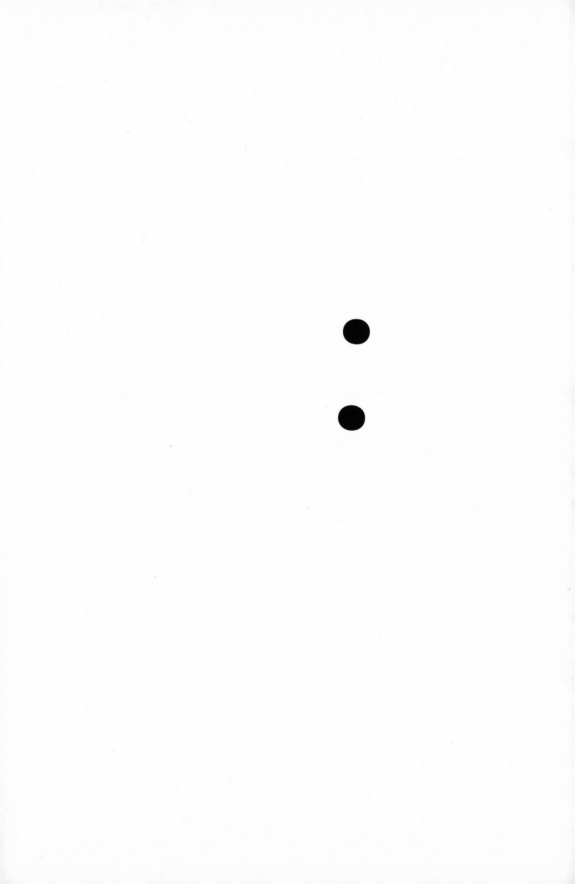

IN GALLERIES

It's places like this, surrounded by edible sculptures, ceramic pelvises, and pieces of other planets, that I think most of my stalker. When I was a teenager I showed my mom a drawing my first girlfriend gave me of Kermit the Frog. He had two cacti growing out of his head. The caption read, "I fuck pigs." My mom said her friends would have been too afraid of offending each other to exchange such things.

In places my stalker would never venture, I'm most aware I'm being pursued, places like the parking garage where my first girlfriend and I covered an office chair with tinsel and spun each other around until it collapsed, wondering if we were making art. We slept in the same bed every night for a year before I even got to touch her tits, which for that year, like me, were composed entirely of wondering. Now, both of us having all the sex we want with people far better suited for us, we sit in bars talking about insurance.

When we met we played Judas Priest on screeching 45 under a table, eating cake with our hands that we had baked secret messages into. I wanted to kiss her like I wanted my next breath, but I couldn't—I felt something bad might happen, like somehow I would be followed.

WAX FRUIT

I know spring has arrived because in the park by my apartment my stalker has taken her sweater off. She comes to the park every day. In her country, this is how you convince someone you love them more than your own life. In my country, where we are both citizens, it's diagnosable. The distance from my window to where she is standing is the least magical kind of black magic, like a piece of wax fruit.

MOST DUST HAS BEEN AT A PARTY

Because I expected everyone around me not to melt into rotting sacks of diseases and hair extensions, my expectations were too high, and I experienced disappointment. I'd known they were some kind of melting sacks, but from the outside their contents appeared to have a pleasing consistency. I tell this tiny perfect woman she is the only person I've ever seen look good in only socks and a T shirt, and I mean it, but words seem increasingly like invisible or possibly liquid increments of measurement. I was listening to the sounds of laughter and Harry Belafonte fade as I walked away from a wedding through a dark parking lot, and the words I thought I heard were "seize the day," but I had drunk too much of this blue vodka, and I was drenched in bad perfume, and I was walking through the dark alone after a wedding. I wonder if that is what dying feels like—the dust of a nighttime parking lot on your lips as somebody else's party gets farther away.

INTERNET PICTURE

A naked man with Pokemon underwear
stretched over his face, eyes rolled back,
the cotton crotch taut against his mouth.
He makes an ornate building seem inevitable.
What other increment of measurement exists
for the distance between what is inside
that panting head and what's outside it?

It's a pretty increment—
arches of bricks around its windows
like embroidery, blossoms of concrete
under eaves high enough to shadow
the whole street and everything
that happens there.

Crazed by fantasy, one hauls concrete
and re-bar across the world just to see oneself,
any part of oneself here. Cross-eyed
at the bar I said, "I want to touch you
the way you touch yourself."

You called me crude, and I am—
filthy as my browser history,
and often less interesting,
but I thought of each perfect word
you breathed in my ear,

photo negatives of cathedrals
I don't have to build,
how far from your bed
my bricks can rest.

MY INTERNET DATING PROFILE

I'm late for a date because I'm watching a video
of a chimpanzee fucking a frog,
but I say it's because I couldn't decide what to wear.

As we squeeze each other's adrenaline-damp hands
I can't explain the video and I certainly don't explain
its relevance to the moment.

In oblivious bliss the chimp thrusts into the frog's mouth,
everything no one wants to admit about that lauded quality,
innocence. The frog's encounter with

an organism so much more complex than itself
that it barely survives
is what I imagine it's like to meet god.

On the horizon the ocean's lightbulb filament-blaze
swallows the sun, the soft sand is millions of years
of pulverized life. Her tongue is a broom in

a drunken Fred Astaire imitation. I draw it into my mouth
and then fill hers. To whatever extent I have a "type,"
it's that video.

I DON'T KNOW ANYTHING
AND NEITHER DO YOU

If you're going to be in my room insisting you know
something, you better be naked and bent over like me. We'll
stare at the floor, feeling educated and important as the draft
from the kitchen makes us colder and colder.

THE SEX-ADDICTED PRISM

I asked for skim milk because whole milk turns me on.

So do whipping creams, walks on the beach,
walkers, wheelchairs, Hot Wheels,
quicksand, topless bars, topping bars,
the Village People, construction workers,
deconstruction, and a certain
intersection near the airport.

The only pictures on my internet dating profile
are of two butts, both of which are mine.
I can see them reflected in your eyes
as you approach me across rooms.
At worst my love is one facet of a prism.

Okay, honestly I asked for skim milk because I've got
one ex who can't stay in a city longer than a week,
one so drunk no chair can keep her upright—
I'm not bragging, I'm refracting.

Every love is a new me that departs too quickly.
Every time you say yes they surround us.
They look like they were dragged under a bus,
but they're dancing.

YOU CAN DETERMINE HOW FAR AWAY A STORM IS BY HOW MUCH THUNDER MISSES LIGHTNING

You were the recipient of my first
drunk question,
"Why don't you have any friends?"

I asked in disbelief—
our conversations felt like dancing,
which I correctly identified as love—
all I could imagine anyone feeling for you then.

In a dark room where everyone watched
Fear and Loathing in Las Vegas
you rolled onto me.

"I'm sorry," you said
and for the first time
my blood levitated.

Yet as in a dream
my body refused
to lift my mouth inches to yours.

43

When I returned to the room
you were in the corner giving
a boy a handjob.

Knowing nothing, I thought
I still had only inches to travel.

Even after a year in your bed
you introduced me as your friend.
My happiest moments before you
touched me were dreams
about flying.

I thought the secret of adulthood
is you find out you can't fly,
but when you fall in love
you become the sky,
fine enough for even
the clouds and the moon to live in.

After finding you
in too many corners with boys,
I gave up
and we were friends.

To my surprise,
I remained the sky.

These days I struggle to hear you
because of the great distance,
and because the moon and clouds
have loud sex and both wear stiletto heels.

ENOUGH TO DROWN IN

The way you were fluorescent on me like the word "fuck" spoken in a Ukrainian accent, your mouth like immortal cowboys beating each other with pieces of the same couch, the rain that made tents of light under the street lamps, all our fancy celebrity parties, though the celebrities only existed as much as the gray light in your room at certain times—I bet none of it would have happened if it weren't for all the coffee. The moats of coffee, the oceans of coffee. I bet people are drinking it right now.

THE ENCHANTED SINUS INFECTION

The phrase "Sour Sour Pinecone Fish" on a restaurant's menu made me laugh so hard hot coffee came out my nose, which was odd because I hadn't been drinking any. It poured out until the entire table was soaked. Several people approached me to ask if a doctor was needed, and I said no. I knew I was discovering how the magic of language manifests itself in my life—as some kind of enchanted coffee sinus infection.

MUFFINS OFF THE FLOOR

It looks like it should have a handle, the way its extreme density causes it to sink to the center of the earth, but that could be said of most of our drunken nights of eating smashed muffins off the floor. We continually attempt to force the nights to have handles, but they're incapable. Their incapability is frustrating, but it assures us that physics is still the clumsy, sexually insatiable dental hygienist we remember so fondly.

BIOLOGY

This isn't tomato soup, this is mushroom soup, which means this is
    the soup that shares the most DNA with humans.

This is the cutest fish in the sea: it adheres best to rough rocks.

This is a dead fish in a harness: it sticks to things in a way that is less
    similar to humans than to tomato soup. Its pelvic fins
    have vanished into a suction cup.

This is limp lobster syndrome, but it gets worse.

This is actually a net cast over the prey cells.

This is a different ciliate: it has a basket for a mouth. It is the mason
    of the microbial world.

Can you imagine violating the size limit of cells?

How can a shark look like it's on a treadmill?

Have you ever picked up a tuna? They're very hard to bend.

Have you ever printed a 3D model of a shell and then crushed it?

This is the stomach that's dark to hide bioluminescence.

Look closer: you are stomach all the way down.

WITCH BONER:
FOG IS MY FAVORITE WEATHER

In a dream, Jasmine fucked a woman in a grocery store who was wearing a prepackaged nylon witch costume while yelling, "I'm not gay, this is just my witch boner!" From across the street, my apartment building appears to have unfamiliar additions, columns and turrets and silos jutting out of the walls and roof at impossible angles. Only witch boners could live there. I know because of the way I learned about sex—I was looking out my bedroom window in the house where I grew up, and from that angle the neighbors' yard looked like a wilderness that went on forever. I wanted to go there, but if I turned my head, even slightly, the fence reappeared.

THE INFLATABLE POOL RAFT AT SEA

Not many people accidentally call a phone sex line
when they're trying to reach a suicide prevention hotline,
but when you meet one it's like meeting the president.

It's said some people become politicians
because others inherently defer to them
the way your body defers,

spasmed across town
by the chance the ambulance won't
get there in time,

a dead person you could identify by touch.

Of course she is
drunk, throwing wine glasses at the EMTs,
as usual not being dead in a way
that launched a thousand boats, or at least one stupid boat
that's probably an inflatable pool raft,
she is not being dead with a grandiosity
you could march to.

YOU COMPARE PEOPLE TO LEGOS

As you roll onto a woman I love

in your apartment piled with computers,

it's impossible you know

I just woke up alone after

dreaming she and I saw

a soccer player die on the field.

His body was unceremoniously liquefied

in a giant blender

and flushed down a toilet.

It's possible you know I hate

soccer and she loves it,

but not that the argument we had

about this in the dream

was so plausible, when I woke up

I wished I could still call her.

CONFESSIONAL

Is it worrisome that I like digging up dead bodies and putting sunglasses on them more than I like IPAs? I tried burying an IPA and then digging it up once, in hopes that I'd like it more, but the sunglasses didn't fit and it was still too bitter and hoppy. I love porters, but I love them so much I'm actually ashamed. You are the first person I've ever admitted this to.

SENIOR HOUSING

I can't remember why Tim drew a dick he had seen that resembled a Christmas tree, though I clearly remember that he drew ornaments on it. "Identity" is memories, a growing collection of Christmas tree dick ornament memories without reason, which make something as reasonable as a "home" seem like a completely inappropriate container for old people.

PERSPECTIVE

I don't feel very comfortable wearing makeup, but I also don't feel comfortable when a blood-covered clown comes out of the shower drain.

<3

For years I believed
the famous Edgewater Hotel mud shark incident
was when all of the members of Led Zeppelin
gang-banged a shark.
This isn't true and you should not research
what really happened. I also believed

heart emojis were pointy erections,
and complimented the sex
drive of the woman who
most often sent them to me, who
laughed until she barfed out the window.

The only person I know who shares
this misconception is Riley,
who I first saw driving
a 1964 Buick Electra four-door hardtop
with a bumper sticker that said "Follow me
to the moon!"

I got in that car, its stated voyage
made impossible partly by its

beauty, even more impossible

by the weight of an additional astronaut,

and we keep driving,

watching the stars whiz by.

YOU DESERVE AN ENTOURAGE

You deserve an entourage, and anyone who doesn't see that can set their dick on fire. I'm assembling your entourage now, because I want a turkey in my pants. Nothing smothers flames like a whole raw turkey. What I mean, of course, is that I believe in you.

BOOBS BOOBS BOOBS
SCREAMING JAY HAWKINS

Language makes it possible to outline meanings that are impossible to express directly, creating for a moment an illusory sense of owning them. This is why I hate naming poems. Meanings that can be stated directly are unworthy of ownership, and naming something forces one to express what it "is." For this reason I have decided to simply name poems after other things I like. If I had to name this poem, I would call it, "Boobs Boobs Boobs Screaming Jay Hawkins."

ROMANTIC COMEDY

Don't worry, just like UFOs and the Four Horsemen of the Apocalypse, Hugh Grant is nothing more than a hoax. It was not a religious miracle that his image appeared in a pancake—it was simple biology. That is how pancakes reproduce.

PEEP SHOW

"Why does this even exist?" read the caption below a photo of a flower on social media. The caption was a joke, but in an age when everything has a bird on it, the sentiment was refreshing. Birds are probably great, but the best peeps are silent, be they glimpses of nudity or marshmallows. Does anyone ornamented with images of wolves or owls even know these animals are not marshmallows? To be honest, the only time I've been totally convinced birds aren't marshmallows was when I witnessed two male pigeons mating and was legitimately turned on. Directly obtaining a resource from another organism was so alarming I had to dress up as a combine harvester immediately.

THE HUMAN BUBBLE BATH

I don't know who I am,
but sometimes I feel like a human bubble bath,
and sometimes I feel like a priest.

I was making out with a girl on the bus once,
and a drunk guy yelled, "Get a room, you priests!"
I don't know why he called us priests,
but I hope I am one,

just because of how it felt on that bus,
where the fog of collective heat on the windows
barely muted deep blue air that shows nothing,

and me imagining I might be something,
and that there might even be two of us.

THE POOR MAN'S TELEPORTATION

Between the sight of a woman dressed in black and gold-embroidered velvet putting a Roy Orbison song on the jukebox and me handing her a coaster with my phone number on it

there was some kind of distance, but not one I could see or feel.

If sex is the poor man's opera, perhaps this is the poor man's teleportation?

She told me later she brought me a "corsage," then placed in my coat pocket a mummified turkey leg, and then we were on a rooftop listening to Roy Orbison through a shared set of headphones.

When I was a kid my mom told me that Proust saw a girl in a garden who he never spoke to, and that he was in love with her the rest of his life.

My mom hated Proust, poor guy.

The most glamorous image I ever saw was a black-and-white photo of my aunt and uncle on their way to a party.

Even after they divorced, I wondered if there was a suit like his that would fit me.

She showed me her fake tooth, and I showed her the tooth the dentist pulled out, which I pinned to my jacket with a safety pin. We had survived nearly identical car accidents.

After she left for work I lay in bed staring into something that could not have been space

because it was full.

I looked into what T.S. Eliot called the heart of light, while I thought of Little Richard singing,

"When she walks by, a bread slice turns to toast."

When I looked at my digital watch the emblem of a jogger on the screen had turned into a witch riding a broom,

and though my finger trembled, god damn was I going to push that button.

THE HOUSE MADE OF WHALES

I dreamed you told me you saw a house made of whales. "Even the shower was made of whales," you said. According to some antiquated methods of dream interpretation, I probably had this dream because of the plastic whale-shaped pool toy we had sex with in the shower last night until it deflated, but any credible contemporary psychologist would say that never happened and let's never speak of it again.

BLACK FRIDAY

Your gold mirrored coffee table is the most beautiful I've seen
except for the one I break with my dick every year at Christmas.
It's actually a series of IKEA tables I discard afterward,
but the power of tradition to beautify is practically endless.

I LIVE IN AN ACTUAL FLOPHOUSE

built for destitute men in the 1920s,
although it's 2015 and I'm
made entirely of expensive marble,
especially my enormous breasts.
This may explain why,
as my first romantic gesture to you,
I played a song called "Party Time,"
which is about an orgy of grandparents
at a family reunion.
See: it isn't true that stone hearts
are always cold, as anyone
who has smelled rain
on summer freeways knows.
My weird mineral heart
sincerely loves reunions.

GOD'S PLAN

I'll finally achieve financial security as a drug-dealing cockney chimney sweep. Who can resist a cheeky, soot-covered urchin who swoops down the chimney with a bag of cocaine? I'll expand my business into a drug-dealing cockney chimney sweep service. I'll keep it independent, with full benefits and paid vacations for all employees. To market to consumers more comfortable with big corporations, I'll require all employees to continuously drink human blood while on the job. The business will finance my dream of living in a network of bouncy castles and never dying and having three pairs of breasts like an opossum.

YOUR NAME EMBROIDERED ON IT

There will be a meteor shower at 3 A.M.,
this Kate Bush album is good,
Nick, who I sort of knew, died yesterday—
I tell you anything.

I told you when a guy in Pioneer Square
yelled at me, "Someone just died back there!"
I heard sirens, then he added, "Ya got a nice butt!"

I could think of no better response to death.

I told you that when Nick died I pulled his old bag,
embroidered with his nickname, "Fingers,"
from under my bed and cried,
thinking of a painting he made
of a refrigerator with a forest inside it.

I told you the lace of peeling gray paint
surrounding an electrical meter
which no one else would notice but you
made me feel like a moderately-priced car
rattling from outrageously
loud, clear speakers.

All these words would be depleted by your absence
like the word "Fingers" on that bag.

I could walk around complimenting strangers' butts,
except "butts" would mean something different if you died,
and so would "compliments."

I wouldn't know what to pull from under my bed
or put back.

EVERYONE'S SEXY THIS MONTH

Why cry about how fucked up your family is when you can use their twelve most dysfunctional moments as themes for an erotic calendar? The time your mom hit your dad in the face with a liquor bottle, then in a fit of remorse retrieved it and bashed herself until she got a concussion could be great for July, because of the barbecue and the smell you remember that might have been fireworks. When phenobarbital convinced your grandma a LITTLE glass was okay in the turkey—November, obviously. You can do sort of a bondage thing for the month your brother was dragged away by the FBI after his child porn website got busted. You won't even need models for January, the month you noticed your twin uncles shower together—they've aged remarkably well. For April, the month you were born, an image of you alone, masturbating, repeated infinitely as if viewed through a kaleidoscope.

PASTAPHILIA

At a party in a century-old train car,

we dance on the table, stepping in cake,

knocking over glasses.

Everyone present agrees this train car,

which once belonged to FDR, is among the few

beautiful things left in town.

We thrash in its fringe curtains,

which resemble sheets of gold noodles,

until the dust flies from them,

yelling "PASTAPHILIA!" in fake Italian accents

and I wonder what it is about new snow

that makes me run through it.

Later in our bed

I touch you everywhere,

looking for the damage.

GOD DOESN'T CARE WHERE YOU PEE

It must have been fun designing the hypno-toad,

but since I'm not god,

the last thing I designed was a quesadilla

which had limited hypnotic properties.

For instance, my mom designated the woman I made

the quesadilla for as "daughter" on social media.

The woman loves me though I'm not a god—

proof that magic exists.

Last night I drank Mickey's until I felt like a cloud

of falling confetti,

thinking of the woeful state of the animals I've assembled.

TACO TIME

Every couple has their Saturday night activity,
like eating a dress made of tacos
off a go-go dancer together.

Addiction is when a person wants every moment
of life to feel that way,

which everyone does.

Our voltage is no lower than other mammals—
pigeons dance and strut after each other
even on footless stumps.

The mind capable of conducting an orchestra
envisions being fucked with every instrument.

Most people die with an entire taco-dress
in their bloodstream, still smiling
at the crash of cymbals on the stereo.

SOMETHING WE
STOMPED OURSELVES

Next time we go to a dinner party we should bring something
we stomped ourselves, like wine we made in the bathtub.

Social media gives people a sense of connection opposite to the one
a dinner party provides, because it involves no dinner.

A dinner party featuring dishes that may or may not be edible
because they're made by processes we probably learned from a cartoon

would combine traditional and contemporary forms of human connection,
resulting in the most fulfilling experience possible.

IT'S ADORABLE HOW MY DENTIST RIDES A DOCTOR TO WORK

It was actually the first thing I noticed about her.
Jem and Sterling, who had been together 51 years,
advised me to pay close attention to first impressions.
They remembered how they laughed
when Jem panicked upon discovering that Sterling,
to whom he admitted he was evading a parking ticket,
was a cop. They remembered each other's laughter,
and (still shyly!) each other's good looks.
From Sterling's death I learned even love's
grand prizes leave one winner alone with a trophy.
Even after their advice led me to a woman who lit up
the oldest gay bar on the West Coast
like lightning on vacation,
I watch what each person I meet says and does.
A full trophy case appeals to my human sensibility,
as at odds with sense as it may be.

THE LANGUAGE OF COME

The saddest thing I've ever learned
is most people's come
is a foreign language,
retaining a fraction of its alien beauty
(if you're lucky)
by the time you've learned
what it means. Or worse,
it is calculus.

Like snow, every orgasm
with my first love turned
the house where I grew up
into a new place
where nothing terrible had happened,

but of course
the best thing about a new
place is meeting new people,
and wherever there is more
than one person,
something terrible happens.

What I mean is I'm not sad
because of you, I just wish
we could kiss
somewhere that isn't melting.

TO BE DAZZLED

I demand that you lie on the sidewalk
next to your own underwear.
I want you to know it
the way I know you,

how I wake up next to you
each morning disoriented, naked,
invincible.

THE PATRON SAINT OF BLOWING UP ROTISSERIE CHICKENS WITH FIREWORKS

I'm in love with the patron saint of blowing up rotisserie chickens with fireworks. She smells like she's on fire and is sometimes too hot to touch, her hair is always full of coleslaw. There is no purpose for the event she's the saint of, but whenever it happens, anywhere on earth, her halo lights up and everything in our vicinity is as beautiful as a renaissance painting. She is the happiest of all the saints.

Ugly Time

Thanks to Georgia Galvin, Tom Kohn, Mike Kohn, Jacob Block, Emily Galvin, James Galvin (my family), Bill True, Drew Scott Swenhaugen, Rich Smith, Piper Daniels, Willie Fitzgerald, Heather McHugh, Cody Walker, Linda Bierds, David Schmader, Bethany Jean Clement, Paul Constant, Leah Baltus, Dan Paulus, Adrian Ryan, Robert Roth, Barbara Osborn, David Schraer, Will Waley, James Gendron, Ed Skoog, Anastacia Tolbert, Monica McClure, Derek Erdman, Stella Rose St. Claire, Jack Bennet, Riley Christiansen, Web Crowell, and Mary Anne Carter, whose love, support and inspiration reminds me of the beauty in everything.

Sarah Galvin is the author of a book of poems,
The Three Einsteins (Poor Claudia, 2014), and
a book of essays, *The Best Party of Our Lives*
(Sasquatch, 2015). Her poetry and essays can
also be found in the *Guardian*, *Vice Magazine*, *io*,
New Ohio Review, and *Pinwheel*, among others.
She is a regular contributor to *City Arts* and *The
Stranger* newspaper. She is a winner of the 2015
Lottery Grant, a 2015 and 2016 James W. Ray
award nominee, and was considered for what
would have been the first Radio Flyer Wagon
DUI in Washington State history.

GRAMMA POETRY